3 4028 07632 5654
HARRIS COUNTY PUBLIC LIBRARY

J 394.261 Fre
Freeman, Dorothy Rhodes
Kwanzaa

$23.93
ocm81150131
Rev. and update   12/15/2010

WITHDRAWN

# KWANZAA

### REVISED AND UPDATED

Dorothy Rhodes Freeman and Dianne M. MacMillan

## Enslow Elementary

an imprint of

## Enslow Publishers, Inc.

40 Industrial Road
Box 398
Berkeley Heights, NJ 07922
USA

http://www.enslow.com

## Acknowledgements

The authors wish to thank the people at the African American Cultural Center of Los Angeles, California, for reviewing the manuscript and for providing information on the Kwanzaa celebration.

Also, our thanks to John Kiango, Swahili Language Instructor at Columbia University, for his review of the Swahili language and pronunciations used in the text.

Enslow Elementary, an imprint of Enslow Publishers, Inc.

Enslow Elementary® is a registered trademark of Enslow Publishers, Inc.

Copyright © 2008 by Enslow Publishers, Inc.

All rights reserved.

No part of this book may be reproduced by any means without the written permission of the publisher.

**Library of Congress Cataloging-in-Publication Data**

Freeman, Dorothy Rhodes.
   Kwanzaa, revised and updated / Dorothy Rhodes Freeman & Dianne M. MacMillan.
     p. cm. — (Best holiday books)
   Includes bibliographical references and index.
   ISBN-13: 978-0-7660-3042-8
   ISBN-10: 0-7660-3042-3
   1.  Kwanzaa—Juvenile literature. 2.  African Americans—Social life and customs—Juvenile literature. I. MacMillan, Dianne M., 1943–    II. Title.
GT4403.F74  2008
394.2612—dc22                           2007002421

Printed in the United States of America

10 9 8 7 6 5 4 3 2

**To Our Readers:** We have done our best to make sure all Internet Addresses in this book were active and appropriate when we went to press. However, the author and the publisher have no control over and assume no liability for the material available on those Internet sites or on other Web sites they may link to. Any comments or suggestions can be sent by e-mail to comments@enslow.com or to the address on the back cover.

**Illustration Credits:** AP, pp. 9, 41; Artville, p. 5; Carlin Photo/Shutterstock, p. 29 (top); Chester Higgins/Photo Researchers, Inc., p. 17; Chris Keane/AP, p. 26 (top); Clipart.com, p. 36; Courtesy of Phillips Academy, © 2006 John Hurley, p. 38; David Romero Corral/Shutterstock, p. 29 (bottom); David P. Smith/Shutterstock, p. 26 (bottom right); Georgy Markov/Shutterstock, p. 35 (bottom left); The Image Works, pp. 1, 28, 39; © 2007 Jupiter Corporation, pp. 26 (bottom left), 34, 35 (top left and bottom right); © Kayte M. Deioma/Photo Edit, p. 4; © Kazuyoshi Nomachi/HAGA/The Image Works, p. 10; Lawrence Migdale/Photo Researchers, Inc., p. 31; Library of Congress, p. 27; Nina Shannon/ Shutterstock, p. 21; © Patrick Olear/Photo Edit, p. 22; Shutterstock, pp. 3, 19, 26 (bottom left background), 35 (top right); Terry White/istockphoto.com, pp. 11, 33.

**Cover Photo:** The Image Works

# Contents

These boys are playing traditional African drums during a Kwanzaa celebration in Long Beach, California.

# THE HOLIDAY KWANZAA

\*

KWANZAA (**KWAHN**-ZAH) IS AN AFRICAN-American holiday. It lasts seven days. The first day is December 26. The last day is January 1. It celebrates the African past of black people. It is also about their life in America.

Kwanzaa is a time for families. Families spend time together every day. People wear bright African-style clothing. They eat

MEDITERRANEAN SEA

Morocco

Tunisia

Algeria

Libya

Egypt

Western Sahara

Mauritania

Mali

Niger

Chad

Sudan

Eritrea

Senegal
① ②
Guinea
③
④
Côte D'Ivoire
Burkina Faso
⑥ ⑤
Ghana
Nigeria
Benin
Cameroon
Central African Republic
Ethiopia
Somalia

⑦
Gabon
⑧
Democratic Republic of the Congo
Uganda
⑨ ⑩
Kenya
Rwanda
Burundi
Tanzania

Atlantic Ocean

Angola
Zambia
⑪
Mozambique
Zimbabwe
Madagascar
Namibia
Botswana
⑫
South Africa
⑬

① The Gambia
② Guinea-Bissau
③ Sierra Leone
④ Liberia
⑤ Togo
⑥ Benin
⑦ Equatorial Guinea
⑧ Republic of the Congo
⑨ Rwanda
⑩ Burundi
⑪ Malawi
⑫ Swaziland
⑬ Lesotho

N W E S

AFRICA

The continent of Africa includes about fifty countries!

African food and listen to African music. They talk about their grandparents and great-grandparents.

The word "kwanza" is Swahili. Swahili is an African language that many Africans understand. In Swahili, kwanza means "first." It stands for the first fruits picked at harvest-time.

This holiday began in 1966. At that time, a holiday program was planned by Dr. Maulana Karenga. Seven children wanted to hold signs spelling Kwanza. But there were only six letters. An "a" was added to Kwanza. The holiday's name became Kwanzaa. Each child had a letter to hold.

> The Swahili word "kwanza" stands for the first fruits picked at harvest-time.

Maulana Karenga started Kwanzaa to bring people together.

# HOW KWANZAA BEGAN

\*

DR. MAULANA KARENGA IS AN AFRICAN-American leader. He teaches at California State University at Long Beach. In the 1960s, he thought that African Americans did not know about their history. He wanted them to be proud of their past. He also thought that African Americans needed to build stronger families.

Part of the Nuba Tribe in Sudan celebrates the corn harvest.

He wanted families to share ideas and grow closer. Dr. Karenga decided to start a holiday that would meet these goals.

First he studied many groups of African people. In every group there was a "first fruits," or harvest, holiday. The holidays were called different names. But in every holiday people did some of

the same things. They came together.
They thanked God for giving them food
and a good life. They remembered their
parents, grandparents, aunts, and uncles
who had died. They judged how they lived
the past year. They made plans for the
new year. They sang, danced, and ate food
together.

Dr. Karenga wanted Kwanzaa to be
like harvest holidays in Africa. Some of
those holidays lasted three days. Some
lasted nine days. Most
of them were seven
days long. Dr. Karenga
liked having a seven
day holiday. One group
of people from the
southern part of Africa
had a holiday at the
end of the year. They

> Dr. Karenga wanted
> Kwanzaa to be like
> African harvest holidays.

celebrated for seven days until the new
year began. Dr. Karenga thought this
would be good for Kwanzaa.

The table is set for Kwanzaa with a mat, a kinara, a cup, some corn, and a basket of fruit.

# SEVEN
# DAYS

\*

DR. KARENGA FOUND THAT MANY AFRICAN groups followed seven principles, or rules. He decided to use one of these for each day of Kwanzaa. By the end of the week, all seven principles would be covered.

The seven principles are called Nguzo Saba (NA-GOO-zoo SAH-bah). "Nguzo" means "principles." Saba means "seven."

Each day of Kwanzaa, families come together. They do some things Africans did in the African holiday. They also talk about one important principle each day.

Before the holiday begins, the family gets everything ready. They put a straw mat on a table. On top of the mat they put a candleholder with seven candles. Each candle stands for one of the principles.

Each day a candle will be lit. The one in the center is black. Three candles on one side are red. The three candles on the other side are green. The colors have meaning. The black candle is for the African American people. The red is for their struggles, now and in the past. Green is for their hopes for the future.

Then the family puts a basket of fruit and vegetables, some ears of corn, and a cup on the table. Next to these there are some gifts for the children. Each of these

Each one of the seven candles stands for a different principle of Kwanzaa.

things stands for an important idea. Now the seven days begin.

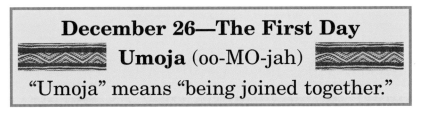

**December 26—The First Day**

**Umoja** (oo-MO-jah)

"Umoja" means "being joined together."

People are united in their feelings. They are together in their ideas. Members of a family feel they belong together.

On the first day of Kwanzaa, a family gets together. Most of the time, this gathering is before the evening meal. But some families have their Kwanzaa ceremony in the morning or in the afternoon. A ceremony is a celebration that is always done the same way.

The family stands by the table with the mat and the candle holder with the seven candles.

When everyone is ready, the black candle is lit. Anyone may light it. The person lighting the candle tells its

**15**

meaning. He or she might say, "Today is the first day of Kwanzaa. I light the black candle. It stands for unity. It means being together. Unity is the most important principle. We must join together in our neighborhood. We need unity in our families. Then we will feel close to one another."

After this, everyone in the family takes a turn speaking. Each one tells why he or she thinks unity is important.

The next part of the Kwanzaa ceremony remembers family members who have died. Someone picks up a cup. The cup is filled with water or fruit juice. First, some of the water or juice is poured into a bowl. This pouring is to honor those family members who have died. Then, the person drinks from the cup. He or she raises the cup high and says, "Harambee" (hah-RAHM-bee).

> "Harambee" means "Let's all pull together."

"Harambee" means "Let's all pull together." That is another way of saying, "Let's all work together."

Everyone says, "Harambee!" Everyone repeats it seven times. Each time is for one of the seven principles. Then the cup is passed around. Each person drinks from it, but in a large group, only the leader drinks from the cup.

Now the names of African American leaders and heroes are called out. The people think about the great things these heroes did.

The ceremony is now finished for the night. It is time to eat. Then the family sings or listens to African music.

Kwanzaa to bring families together. This family is lighting the kinara together.

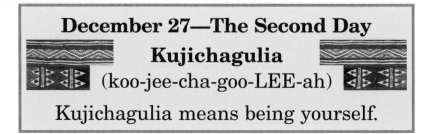

**December 27—The Second Day**
**Kujichagulia**
(koo-jee-cha-goo-LEE-ah)
Kujichagulia means being yourself.

African-American people are to think for themselves. They decide what they will say or do. They do not let other people tell them how to live and what to be.

Everyone is ready for the second night. Another person lights the candles. First the black candle is lit again. Then the second candle, a red one, is lit. The person might say, "I'm going to go to school and learn. I want to be a doctor. Some people will say that I can't do it. But I know I can."

All of the family members share their ideas about doing what they think is right for themselves. Once again the family drinks from the cup. They remember the family members who

Traditional African clothes are an important part of Kwanzaa.

have died. The children love shouting "Harambee" seven times.

Many African Americans like to wear African-style clothes during Kwanzaa. Men and women wear long, loose shirts. Some wear robes. They may wear caps and head wraps. All of the clothes have bright colors.

Long ago, African queens wore their hair in cornrows, or small braids. Some people call them plaits. Many African-American women and girls like to wear their hair this way.

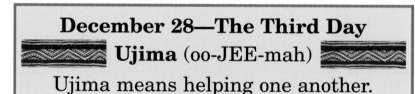

**December 28—The Third Day**
**Ujima** (oo-JEE-mah)
Ujima means helping one another.

People cooperate by working together. They help one another solve problems.

On this day, the black candle and one of the red candles are lit. These are the candles of the first two days. Now the third candle is lit. It is green. The person who lights the candles might say, "All of us need to help one another. If someone needs food or help, we give it. If someone's home burns down, we all help rebuild it. We give the family food and clothes. We help with what we have."

African foods are an important part of Kwanzaa. Plantains are a familiar food in Africa.

The family talks about how they have a duty to help their neighbors. By helping one another, all grow stronger.

After the talk, the family honors relatives who have died. They drink from the cup. Then they eat dinner. Families cook African foods. They might have African chicken stew, fried plantains (similar to bananas), and yams. Often they sit on the floor. They eat food with their fingers. This is the African way.

## December 29—The Fourth Day
## Ujamaa (oo-jah-MAH)
Ujamaa means sharing.

People share the work. They also share the money they make from working.

The candles of the first three nights are lit. Then the fourth candle is lit. It is a red one. Now one black, one green, and two red candles are all burning.

A mom is helping her daughter light the kinara.

Parents like to have the children light the candles. A child gets to be the first one to tell about the principle. This helps him or her remember what the principle means. The child lighting the candles this night might say, "Our class needs some new books. Everyone is going to bring some money. Together we will have enough to buy some books. We can all share them."

The parents might talk about starting a business with some friends. They would share the work and the money. An uncle might share the money from his job with the family. Everyone talks about working and sharing. Then they pour and drink from the cup.

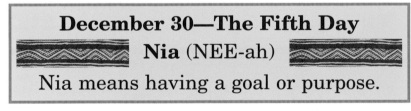

### December 30—The Fifth Day
### Nia (NEE-ah)
Nia means having a goal or purpose.

People need to have goals. They need a purpose or reason for wanting to reach their goals.

On the fifth night, another green candle is lit. Now five candles are burning.

The mother might speak first tonight. She might say, "I think Nia means having a reason to work or having a goal. My goal is to take care of all of you. The purpose of our family is to love and help one another. The goal of Kwanzaa is to help us learn more about who we are. All of us need to set goals. We need to help one another live better lives."

> Each family member tells about the goals they have.

The children might talk about what they want to be when they grow up. One goal of the father might be to help his children get an education so that they can become what they want when they grow up. Others might tell about the goals they have or what purpose means to them.

Talking together about goals helps the family members feel closer. They understand one another better.

Once more they use the cup and remember grandparents and great-grandparents. They talk about the reasons things were done in the past.

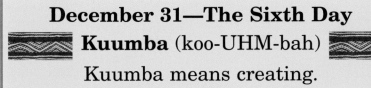

**December 31—The Sixth Day**
**Kuumba** (koo-UHM-bah)
Kuumba means creating.

People create crafts and music and dances. They are also creative when they make their own neighborhoods more beautiful.

The celebrating of the sixth day of Kwanzaa is special. All during the week the family has come together for the Kwanzaa ceremony. On the sixth day, many families join together. They often meet at a community center.

There is a feast called Karamu (kah-RAH-moo). It is a big celebration.

**25**

Community celebrations—including favorite traditional foods—allow many people to come together to celebrate Kwanzaa.

People bring African food to share. There might be peanut soup, collard greens, chicken, fish, black-eyed peas, fruit, and bread.

The room is decorated with black, red, and green banners. A large straw mat is placed on the floor. The candleholder, basket of fruit and vegetables, cup, ears of corn, and gifts are placed on the mat along with plates of food.

The first five candles are lit. Then another red candle is lit. People talk about being creative. Everyone tells what he or she can do or make. They all talk about how they can make their neighborhood more beautiful. A man tells about the chair he fixed. A woman talks about the clothes she is making for her children.

Martin Luther King, Jr., is a famous African American who fought for equality.

People show their creativity through music, plays, dancing, art, storytelling, and poetry. By being creative, people make their lives more beautiful.

Then the ceremony with the cup takes place. Family members are honored and remembered.

Some people call out names of famous African Americans. Someone may give a speech. He or she may talk about heroes like Mary McLeod Bethune, Frederick Douglass, and Martin Luther King, Jr.

These girls are dancing at a Kwanzaa celebration in Philadelphia, Pennsylvania.

After the speech, it is time to share the meal. All help themselves to food. There is always more than enough. This is a happy time with talking and laughing.

After the meal, there is African music and dancing. The dancers wear African clothes. The dances tell stories. Some dances give thanks for the rain and crops.

Some are harvest or victory dances. Music is played on many different drums.

Some families like to sing together. Other families know how to do some of the African dances. There can be music and dances any night of Kwanzaa. There is always music and dancing and the big feast on December 31.

At last, it is time to give the children their gifts. These gifts can be given anytime during Kwanzaa, but most families wait until the sixth day. Children work all year to earn their gifts. They try to remember the seven principles.

Each child receives two gifts. One is always a book. The other gift might be an African picture or carving. It might be something that belonged to a relative.

The West African Djembe drum (left) and the African bongo drums are used for music and dancing during Kwanzaa.

**29**

After the children open their gifts, everyone sings. They are happy to be with one another.

### January 1—The Seventh Day

### Imani (ee-MAH-nee)
Imani means believing.

People need to believe in themselves and other people. They need faith in their future. Many people believe in God.

Imani begins just after Kuumba ends at midnight. It is January 1 of the new year. The singing and the dancing stop. Six candles are already lit. The last candle is lit. Now all seven candles are burning. People talk about what they believe. Some talk about God. They talk about the need to believe in themselves. Children need to believe in their parents, teachers, and leaders.

They talk about the year that has just ended. What mistakes did they make? What can they do in the new year? What goals do they have? What changes will they make?

For the last time, water or juice is poured from the cup. The cup is raised. "Harambee!" Everyone shouts it back seven times.

Kwanzaa is over for the year, but it is not the end of thinking about the seven principles. African Americans who celebrate Kwanzaa try to live by them every day.

The gifts children receive during Kwanzaa reflect the holiday's important principles.

# KWANZAA SYMBOLS

✳

THERE ARE SEVEN THINGS USED AS SYMBOLS during Kwanzaa. They are things people might have in their home. Each one stands for an idea or for people. For Kwanzaa they are given special meanings. They are also given Swahili names.

**Mkeka** (mm-KAY-kah)

The mkeka is a straw mat. It stands for African-American history and ideas.

**Kinara** (kee-NAR-ah)

The kinara is a candle holder. It stands for the family members who have died. It holds seven candles.

**Mishumaa Saba**

(mi-shu-MAH SAH-bah)

Seven candles, called mishumaa saba, are used during Kwanzaa: one black, three red, and three green. They stand for the seven principles.

**Muhindi** (moo-HIN-dee)

Ears of corn are muhindi. They stand for children. One ear of corn is placed on the mat for each child in the family. If there are no children, one ear of corn is still put on the mat. This shows that children are important to everyone.

The kinara holds the seven candles for the Kwanzaa celebration.

## Mazao (mah-ZAH-oh)

Fruits and vegetables are mazao. They stand for the harvest.

## Kikombe Cha Umoja

### (kee-KOHM-bee chah oo-MOH-jah)

Kikombe means cup. The full name means unity cup.

## Zawadi (zah-WAH-dee)

Gifts are zawadi. There are always two gifts given to each child. One must be a book. The other gift can be something from Africa. It could also be something that belonged to a family member.

The flag is an important symbol too. It stands for all African Americans. It has three broad stripes. The colors are black, red, and green. The colors

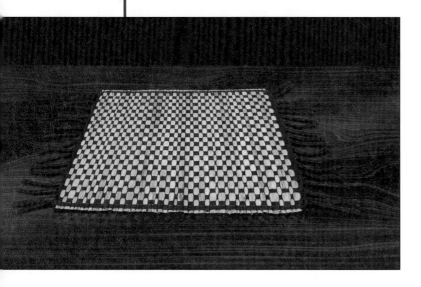

The straw mat is a symbol of the history and culture of African Americans.

The unity cup is to remind everyone that they all want the same things in life.

The fruits and vegetables on the table stand for a good harvest.

Each ear of corn symbolizes one child in the family.

Two gifts are given to each child on the sixth night of Kwanzaa. One is always a book, and the other is something else that is special.

stand for the African-American people, their struggles, and their hopes.

The African-American flag was made by Marcus Garvey. He was a famous African-American leader who lived a long time ago. He made people proud of their African past.

During Kwanzaa, families display the flag. They also decorate their homes with its colors.

This flag was created to symbolize all African Americas. It has the same three colors as the candles in the kinara.

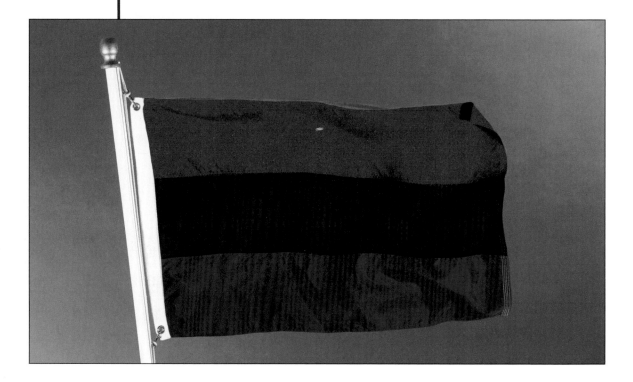

36

# THINGS
# TO DO

\*

THERE ARE MANY THINGS TO SEE AND HEAR during Kwanzaa. Museums show African art. Dancers perform African dances. There are plays and puppet shows about Kwanzaa.

During Kwanzaa, African Americans have a special greeting. They say, "Habari Gani" (ha-BAR-ree GAH-nee). This means "What's new?" A person answers with the principle of the day.

This Kwanzaa ceremony is taking place at Phillips Academy in Andover, Massachusetts.

Sometimes friends send each other Kwanzaa cards. The cards are bright with the three Kwanzaa colors. Some people make their own Kwanzaa cards.

In one city, there is a large Kwanzaa parade. More than two hundred thousand people march in it. Everyone wears African masks and robes. They

**A traditional West African dance highlights a Kwanzaa celebration in Philadelphia, Pennsylvania.**

play African music. As the parade passes, other people join in. Finally the parade ends in a park. There is food and music for everyone.

In other cities, there are classes for children. Some of these classes teach them how to play the drums. Other classes teach them some of the dances.

During December, some children learn about Kwanzaa in their schools. They play African games. They make African crafts and learn about African countries. They talk about how to make the world a better place by using the seven principles.

The first Kwanzaa was celebrated by Dr. Karenga and a few friends. Now millions of African Americans celebrate this holiday. Every year, more people learn about Kwanzaa. African Americans look

Children talk about using the seven principles to make the world a better place.

A storyteller shares stories from Africa, America, and other lands with students in Mississippi.

Now millions of African Americans celebrate Kwanzaa.

forward to the last week of December. It is a time to celebrate learning. It is a time to celebrate pride. It is a time to celebrate sharing. It is also a time for fun and joy. In one of his books, Dr. Karenga wrote, "May the year's end meet us laughing and stronger . . ."

**Harambee! Harambee! Harambee! Harambee! Harambee! Harambee! Harambee!**

# NGUZO SABA— THE SEVEN PRINCIPLES

**Umoja (oo-MO-jah)**—Being united or joined together.

**Kujichagulia (koo-jee-cha-goo-LEE-ah)**—Being yourself. Thinking for yourself; deciding what you are going to do and say.

**Ujima (oo-JEE-mah)**—Working together to help people.

**Ujamaa (oo-jah-MAH)**—Sharing work and wealth.

**Nia (NEE-ah)**—Having purpose or reason for doing something; having a goal.

**Kuumba (koo-UHM-bah)**—Being creative; making something new.

**Imani (ee-MAH-nee)**—Having faith. Believing in people and God.

**ceremony**—A celebration always done in the same way.

**creativity**—Ability to make something new.

**Habari Gani**—Swahili words that mean "What's new?"

**Harambee**—The Swahili word that means "Let's all pull together."

**Karamu**—A Swahili word for the large feast on the sixth day of Kwanzaa.

**kwanza**—The Swahili word that stands for the first fruits picked at harvest time in Africa.

**Kwanzaa**—The African American holiday celebrated each year from December 26 through January 1.

**museum**—A building where things of art, science, or history are kept.

**Nguzo Saba**—The Swahili words for "seven principles." They are used to mean the seven rules of Kwanzaa.

**plantain**—A fruit similar to a banana.

**principle**—A rule of behavior that a person chooses to live by.

**purpose**—The reason for which something is made or done.

**struggle**—To make a great effort, to fight strong opposition.

**Swahili**—An African language spoken in thirteen African countries and understood by many Africans.

**symbol**—A thing that stands for an idea.

⟨◆⟩

## Note to Parents, Teachers, and Librarians

In this book, words within the vocabularies of younger children are used to define the Swahili words. The following list gives the literal meanings of the Swahili terms, as translated by Dr. Maulana Karenga.

**Umoja**—Unity

**Kujichagulia**—Self-determination

**Ujima**—Collective Work and Responsibility

**Ujamaa**—Cooperative Economics

**Nia**—Purpose

**Kuumba**—Creativity

**Imani**—Faith

## Books

Doering, Amanda. *Kwanzaa: African American Celebration of Culture*. Mankato, Minn.: Capstone Press, 2006.

Murray, Julie. *Kwanzaa*. Edina, Minn.: ABDO Pub. Co., 2003.

Nobleman, Marc Tyler. *Kwanzaa*. Minneapolis: Compass Point Books, 2005.

## Internet Addresses

**Kwanzaa: A Celebration of Family, Community and Culture**
http://www.officialkwanzaawebsite.org/index.shtml

**Kwanzaa Activities for Kids**
http://www.apples4theteacher.com/holidays/kwanzaa/

**Kwanzaa Printables**
http://holidays.kaboose.com/kwanzaa-printables.html

# INDEX

**HARRIS COUNTY PUBLIC LIBRARY**
HOUSTON, TEXAS